# EMOTIONALLY
# HEALTHY
# SPIRITUALITY

## WORKBOOK

Emotionally Healthy Spirituality Workbook

# ACKNOWLEDGEMENTS

We want to thank Drew Hyun and Laura Speiller who made significant contributions to the first draft of this workbook. We also want to acknowledge Jim Owens and the feedback from many small groups at New Life Fellowship Church who helped to shape our first edition.

In completing this second edition, we also want to acknowledge the contribution of Parker Palmer's work in leading us to craft more insightful, open-ended questions as well as the "Guidelines for Being Together." This workbook reflects Geri's experience and learnings gleaned from her year of being in a "circle of trust" as part of the Center for Courage and Renewal. We hope this will continue to influence how we do small groups — honoring both our separateness as individuals and togetherness as community.

# TABLE OF CONTENTS

# Introduction

## Welcome

The goal of this workbook is to help you implement the biblical truths found in *Emotionally Healthy Spirituality* (Nelson, 2006). The idea we will unpack is simple yet far-reaching:

> *Emotional health and contemplative spirituality, when interwoven together, offer nothing short of a spiritual revolution, transforming the hidden places deep beneath the surface of our lives.*

Developing emotionally healthy spirituality requires intentionality and intentionality requires a plan. Our prayer is that these studies provide a structure and resources to serve you in carrying out that plan.

Each workbook study on the eight principles explored here could easily have been expanded into its own workbook. This workbook is designed to introduce you to a life with God that goes beyond "tip of the iceberg spirituality" in order that Christ might transform the depths of your being. In fact, the implementation of these pathways will involve the rest of your life.

### The eight studies are broken down as follows:

- **Week 1**: The Problem of Emotionally Unhealthy Spirituality

  **The 7 Pathways to Emotionally Healthy Spirituality**
- **Week 2**: Know Yourself that You May Know God
- **Week 3**: Going Back in Order to Go Forward
- **Week 4**: Journey Through the Wall
- **Week 5**: Enlarge Your Soul Through Grief and Loss
- **Week 6**: Discover the Rhythms of the Daily Office and Sabbath
- **Week 7**: Grow into an Emotionally Mature Adult
- **Week 8**: Go the Next Step to Develop a "Rule of Life"

# How To Use This Workbook

- This workbook has been designed to be most effective when used in conjunction with its companion book, *Emotionally Healthy Spirituality* (Nelson, 2006). You are strongly encouraged to read the designated chapters before each week's study. Although the reading of the book is not absolutely essential to benefit from the studies, it *will* exponentially impact the integration of the material into your life.

- Each of the eight weekly studies is divided into four sections:
  - **Growing Connected**
  - **Starters:** DVD (if using one); and starter question.
  - **Bible Study**: Be sure to bring your Bible.
  - **Applications and Exercises**

- Space is provided throughout the workbook for you to record your answers, questions, responses and other learnings that God may be bringing to you.

- There may be the temptation to spend multiple weeks on each study, but do your best to develop and maintain the *one-meeting/one-study* pace. The workbook is meant to be used as a broad introduction to each of the themes. Remember, the goal is, expressly, to **BEGIN THE JOURNEY** into emotionally healthy spirituality. Seek to complete each study in the time allotted.

- You will notice each study includes the possibility of using a 6–10 minute DVD introduction with Pete Scazzero. It is a very helpful tool, and we encourage you to use it. If you choose not to, be sure to read carefully the introduction provided before each study.

- The "Leader's Notes for Each Study" found in the back of this workbook provides extremely helpful information to supplement the studies. If you are using this workbook on your own, this will also serve you. We especially encourage the leaders/facilitators of groups to avail themselves of this valuable material. All Endnote citations are also found in this section.

# SUGGESTED GUIDELINES FOR THE SMALL GROUP

- **Observe Confidentiality**
  In order to create a safe environment for open and honest sharing only share your own personal experience outside the group. Honor others by keeping what they share personally within the group.

- **Speak for Yourself**
  Use "I" statements as much as possible.

- **Respect Others**
  Be brief in your sharing, being mindful that there are time limitations and others may want to share.

- **Turn to Wonder**
  If you feel judgmental or defensive when someone else is sharing, ask yourself, "I wonder what brought her/him to this belief?" "I wonder what he/she is feeling right now?" "I wonder what my reaction teaches me about myself."

- **Attendance**
  We will begin on time and end on time.

- **Be Prepared**
  To get the most out of our time together, we ask that you read the corresponding chapters in *Emotionally Healthy Spirituality* that go with each study. Be sure to bring your Bible and workbook each week.

- **Silence**
  It is okay to have silence between responses as the group shares, giving members the opportunity to reflect. Remember, there is no pressure to share.

# Week 1

## The Problem of Emotionally Unhealthy Spirituality

## WEEK 1

### The Problem of Emotionally Unhealthy Spirituality

#### READING: CHAPTERS 1, 2, 3

Emotional health and spiritual maturity cannot be separated. It is impossible to be spiritually mature while remaining emotionally immature. We know. We tried — unsuccessfully for years.

When we ignore the emotional component of our lives, we move through the motions of Christian disciplines, activities and behaviors, but deeply rooted behavioral patterns from our past continue to keep us from living an authentic life of maturity in Christ.

We often fail to reflect on what is going on inside us, and around us, (emotional health) and are too busy to slow down to be with God (contemplative spirituality). As a result, we run the high risk of remaining spiritual infants, failing to develop into spiritually and emotionally mature adults in Christ.

Jay, one of our church members, described it best: "I was a Christian for twenty-two years. But instead of being a twenty-two-year-old Christian, I was a one-year-old Christian twenty-two times! I just kept doing the same things over and over and over again."

# THE PROBLEM OF EMOTIONALLY UNHEALTHY SPIRITUALITY

## Growing Connected . . . . . . . . . . . . . . . . . . . . . .20 minutes

1. Share your name, what you hope to get out of the group, and a few words about what makes you feel fully alive.

2. Read aloud the guidelines for your small group from page 7.

## Starters . . . . . . . . . . . . . . . . . . . . . . . . . . . . .20 minutes

*If using the DVD introduction, play it now.*

The following are the top ten symptoms of Emotionally Unhealthy Spirituality. Have the group take turns reading the list aloud and then share the one symptom that is most relevant in your life today.[1]

### 1. Using God to run from God

(e.g. My prayers are usually about God doing my will, not me surrendering to his will).

### 2. Ignoring the emotions of anger, sadness, and fear

(e.g. I am rarely honest with myself and/or others about the feelings, hurts and pains beneath the surface of my life).

### 3. Dying to the wrong things

(e.g. I tend to deny healthy, God-given desires and pleasures of life [friendships, joy, music, beauty, laughter, nature] while finding it difficult to die to my self-protectiveness, defensiveness, a lack of vulnerability and judgmentalism).

### 4. Denying the past's impact on the present

(e.g. I rarely consider how my family of origin and significant people/events from my past have shaped my present).

### 5. Dividing life into "secular" and "sacred" compartments

(e.g. I easily compartmentalize God to "Christian activities" while usually forgetting about him when I am working, shopping, studying or recreating).

### 6. Doing for God instead of being with God

(e.g. I tend to evaluate my spirituality based on how much I am doing for God).

### 7. Spiritualizing away conflict

(e.g. In the name of "peacemaking", we bury tensions and avoid conflict rather than speak the truth in love).

### 8. Covering over brokenness, weakness, and failure

(e.g. Instead of humility and approachability, I am highly reactive and defensive).

### 9. Living without limits

(e.g. Those close to me would say that I often "try to do it all" or "bite off more than I can chew").

### 10. Judging the spiritual journeys of others

(e.g. I often find myself occupied and bothered by the faults of others).

# THE PROBLEM OF EMOTIONALLY UNHEALTHY SPIRITUALITY

## Bible Study — 1 Samuel 15:7-24 . . . . . . . . . . . .30 minutes

Saul, king of Israel, was instructed by God to fight and completely destroy the Amalekites.[2] He succumbed, however, to the wishes of his fighting men and did only part of God's will due to a lack of self-awareness (emotional health) and attentiveness toward God (contemplation). Read 1 Samuel 15:7-24.

1. Verse 11 describes God's and Samuel's response to Saul's actions. What about their response impacts you?

.................................................................................................

.................................................................................................

.................................................................................................

.................................................................................................

2. How does this differ from Saul's response in verse 12 and 13?

.................................................................................................

.................................................................................................

.................................................................................................

.................................................................................................

3. What might have been going on beneath the surface of Saul's life (iceberg) that he was unaware of?[3]

.................................................................................................

.................................................................................................

.................................................................................................

.................................................................................................

4. Reread vv.22-23. Describe in your own words how Samuel explains Saul's disobedience?

..........................................................................................................

..........................................................................................................

..........................................................................................................

..........................................................................................................

..........................................................................................................

..........................................................................................................

5. What are some examples of how we go through the motions of making "burnt offerings" and "sacrifices" rather than "obeying the voice of the Lord"?

..........................................................................................................

..........................................................................................................

..........................................................................................................

..........................................................................................................

..........................................................................................................

..........................................................................................................

6. Note the seriousness of v.23a. What positive step(s) could Saul have taken to become aware of his own iceberg and hear God in his situation? What might be one positive step for you?

..........................................................................................................

..........................................................................................................

..........................................................................................................

..........................................................................................................

..........................................................................................................

..........................................................................................................

## Applications/Exercises .................. 20 minutes

Not only was Saul unaware of what was going on inside of him (emotional health), he also did not cultivate a contemplative life with God (unlike David). His "doing" for God did not flow from his "being" with God.

In the same way, our "doing" for Jesus must flow from our "being" with him. Far too often, we live vicariously off other people's spirituality and relate to God while busily "on the run".

1. What challenges keep you from slowing down your life to be with God?

..................................................................................................................

..................................................................................................................

..................................................................................................................

..................................................................................................................

..................................................................................................................

..................................................................................................................

This diagram illustrates our spiritual life where our activities (e.g., our doing) are out of balance with our contemplative life (e.g, our inner life with Jesus).

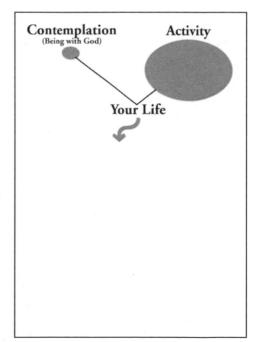

Contemplation
(Being with God)

Activity

Your Life

2. Using two circles like the ones to the right, draw your own diagram to illustrate how your activities (i.e. your doing) balance with your contemplative life (i.e., your being with God).[4]

3. The remainder of the workbook will address the ways we can make changes in our lives. At this point, what might be one or two simple decisions that you can make towards taking a first step to slow down your life and balance your two circles?

..................................................................................................................

..................................................................................................................

..................................................................................................................

..................................................................................................................

..................................................................................................................

..................................................................................................................

..................................................................................................................

..................................................................................................................

..................................................................................................................

..................................................................................................................

..................................................................................................................

..................................................................................................................

..................................................................................................................

..................................................................................................................

..................................................................................................................

..................................................................................................................

..................................................................................................................

..................................................................................................................

..................................................................................................................

..................................................................................................................

4. Take a few minutes and pray together about what God has said to you during this first study.

............................................................................................................

............................................................................................................

............................................................................................................

............................................................................................................

............................................................................................................

............................................................................................................

............................................................................................................

............................................................................................................

............................................................................................................

............................................................................................................

............................................................................................................

............................................................................................................

............................................................................................................

............................................................................................................

............................................................................................................

............................................................................................................

............................................................................................................

............................................................................................................

............................................................................................................

## For Next Week's Study

*Read Chapter 4, "Know Yourself That You May Know God."*

## JOURNAL

# WEEK 2

## KNOW YOURSELF
## THAT YOU MAY

## KNOW GOD

## WEEK 2

### Know Yourself That You May Know God[5]
#### READING: CHAPTER 4

An awareness of yourself is intricately related to your relationship with God. In fact, the challenge to shed our "old false" self in order to live authentically in our "new true" self strikes at the very core of true spirituality.

In AD 500, Augustine wrote in *Confessions,* "How can you draw close to God when you are far from your own self?" He prayed: "Grant, Lord, that I may know myself that I may know thee."

John Calvin, in 1530, wrote in his opening of the *Institutes of the Christian Religion*: "Our wisdom . . . consists almost entirely of two parts: the knowledge of God and of ourselves. But as these are connected together by many ties, it is not easy to determine which of the two precedes and gives birth to the other."

The vast majority of us go to our graves without knowing who we are. Without being fully aware of it, we live someone else's life, or at least someone else's expectations for us. This does violence to ourselves, our relationship with God, and ultimately to others.

**Growing Connected** . . . . . . . . . . . . . . . . . . . . . . .**15 minutes**

1. Describe your dream job. (Remind the group that each person has about 30 seconds to share).[6]

.........................................................................................

.........................................................................................

.........................................................................................

**Starters** . . . . . . . . . . . . . . . . . . . . . . . . . . . . . . .**20 minutes**

*If using the DVD introduction, play it now.*

**Read the following introduction aloud:**

The journey of genuine transformation to emotionally healthy spirituality begins with a commitment to allow yourself to feel. Feelings are an essential part of our humanity and unique personhood as men and women created in God's image. Scripture reveals God as an emotional being who feels as a person. Having been created in his image, we also were created with the gift to feel and experience emotions. Some of us may have learned that feelings are not to be trusted; that they are dangerous and can lead us away from God's will for us. While it is true that we are not to be led by our emotions, they do serve a critical function in our discipleship and discernment of God's will.[7]

Different Aspects/Components
of Who We Are

There are hundreds of emotions, each with their variations, blends, and nuances. Researchers have classified them into eight main families as shown in the following question.

# KNOW YOURSELF THAT
## YOU MAY KNOW GOD

**Allow seven minutes for this question:**

1. Choose four questions from the list below and journal your answers
in the space provided below. If you start journaling and find that there
is a lot to write about on one particular feeling, then simply stay with
that one for the allotted time.

• What are you angry about?

........................................................................................................................

........................................................................................................................

........................................................................................................................

........................................................................................................................

........................................................................................................................

........................................................................................................................

• What are you sad about?

........................................................................................................................

........................................................................................................................

........................................................................................................................

........................................................................................................................

........................................................................................................................

........................................................................................................................

• What are you afraid of?

........................................................................................................................

........................................................................................................................

........................................................................................................................

........................................................................................................................

........................................................................................................................

........................................................................................................................

# KNOW YOURSELF THAT YOU MAY KNOW GOD

• What are you enjoying?

......................................................................................................

......................................................................................................

......................................................................................................

......................................................................................................

......................................................................................................

......................................................................................................

• What (whom) do you love?

......................................................................................................

......................................................................................................

......................................................................................................

......................................................................................................

......................................................................................................

• What are you surprised by?

......................................................................................................

......................................................................................................

......................................................................................................

......................................................................................................

......................................................................................................

• What disgusts you?

......................................................................................................

......................................................................................................

......................................................................................................

......................................................................................................

......................................................................................................

# KNOW YOURSELF THAT YOU MAY KNOW GOD

**Allow eight minutes for this question:**

2. What was it like to journal your feelings?[8]

........................................................................

........................................................................

........................................................................

........................................................................

........................................................................

........................................................................

........................................................................

........................................................................

........................................................................

........................................................................

........................................................................

........................................................................

........................................................................

........................................................................

........................................................................

........................................................................

........................................................................

........................................................................

........................................................................

........................................................................

# KNOW YOURSELF THAT
# YOU MAY KNOW GOD

## Bible Study — 1 Samuel 17:26-45 . . . . . . . . . . .35 minutes

In this famous story, the army of Israel faces the great army of the
Philistines. For forty days, Goliath, described as nine feet tall and dressed
in powerful weaponry, challenges any Israelite soldier to come out and
fight him. When the Israelites saw him, however, "they all ran from him
in great fear" (1 Samuel 17:24 NIV). We pick up the story after David
hears, for the first time, Goliath's humiliating challenge to Israel's army.
Read 1 Samuel 17:26-45.

1. In your own words, what question does David ask after hearing
Goliath's challenge (v.26)?

.................................................................................................

.................................................................................................

.................................................................................................

.................................................................................................

2. What are some of the challenges, accusations and messages
David is getting from the people around him:

• From David's family (v.28)

.................................................................................................

.................................................................................................

.................................................................................................

.................................................................................................

.................................................................................................

• From Saul (v.33, 38)

.................................................................................................

.................................................................................................

.................................................................................................

.................................................................................................

• From Goliath (vv.41-45)?

........................................................................................

........................................................................................

........................................................................................

........................................................................................


3. What feelings might you be experiencing if you were David? For example, what feelings might you have towards your sibling? Towards a person in authority over you like Saul? Towards a Goliath?

........................................................................................

........................................................................................

........................................................................................

........................................................................................


4. How does David live out his true self against the powerful forces and pressures that seek to mold him into someone he is not?

........................................................................................

........................................................................................

........................................................................................

........................................................................................


5. David's ability to be true to himself in the midst of great trials and pressures is, in modern terminology, called **differentiation**.[9] If David had been less differentiated, how might he have responded to his brothers, Saul and Goliath?

........................................................................................

........................................................................................

........................................................................................

## Applications/Exercises . . . . . . . . . . . . . . . . . . . .25 minutes

1. What forces and pressures from circumstances and people cause you to shrink back in fear or "wear armor" that does not fit your true self?

....................................................................................................

....................................................................................................

....................................................................................................

....................................................................................................

....................................................................................................

....................................................................................................

....................................................................................................

2 . Many of us are so unaccustomed to distinguishing our true self from our false self that it may seem difficult to know where to begin. Complete the following sentence and share it with your small group as a first step: I am beginning to realize about myself...

....................................................................................................

....................................................................................................

....................................................................................................

....................................................................................................

....................................................................................................

....................................................................................................

....................................................................................................

....................................................................................................

....................................................................................................

3. Conclude this session prayerfully asking that you may know yourself that you might know God.

.........................................................................

.........................................................................

.........................................................................

.........................................................................

.........................................................................

.........................................................................

.........................................................................

.........................................................................

.........................................................................

.........................................................................

.........................................................................

.........................................................................

.........................................................................

.........................................................................

.........................................................................

.........................................................................

## For Next Week's Study

*Read Chapter 5, "Going Back in Order to Go Forward."*

# WEEK 3
## GOING BACK IN ORDER TO GO FORWARD

## WEEK 3

### Going Back in Order to Go Forward
#### READING: CHAPTER 5

Emotionally healthy spirituality involves embracing God's choice to birth us into a particular family, in a particular place, at a particular moment in history.

That choice to embrace our past grants us certain opportunities and gifts. It also hands us a certain amount of what I will call "emotional baggage" in our journey through life. For some of us this load is minimal; for others, it is a heavy burden to carry.

True spirituality frees us to live joyfully in the present. Living joyfully, however, requires going back in order to go forward. This process takes us to the very heart of spirituality and discipleship in the family of God—breaking free from the destructive sinful patterns of our past to live the life of love that God intends.

# GOING BACK IN ORDER TO GO FORWARD

**Growing Connected** . . . . . . . . . . . . . . . . . . . . . .5 minutes

At our last meeting we studied David and the theme of "Knowing Yourself that You May Know God". This week our topic looks at the very heart of our discipleship in the family of God — "Going Back in Order to Go Forward".

1. How would you describe the family atmosphere you grew up in? (e.g. affirming, complaining, critical, approachable, angry, tense, cooperative, competitive, close, distant, fun, serious, etc.)

......................................................................

......................................................................

......................................................................

**Starters** . . . . . . . . . . . . . . . . . . . . . . . . . . . . . .15 minutes

*If using the DVD introduction, play it now.*

Our need to go back in order to go forward can be summed up in two essential biblical truths:

- The blessings and sins of our families going back two to three generations profoundly impact who we are today.

- Discipleship requires putting off the sinful patterns of our family of origin and re-learning how to do life God's way in God's family.

1. What is your greatest fear in looking back at your family of origin to discern unhealthy patterns and themes? Explain.

......................................................................

......................................................................

......................................................................

# GOING BACK IN ORDER TO GO FORWARD

## Bible Study — Genesis 50:15-21 . . . . . . . . . . . . .35 minutes

The "family" is an emotional system of two to four generations who move through life together in different places at different times. When we are born into families, we inherit their ways of relating, their values, and their ways of living in the world. Your family's story and your individual story cannot be separated.

Joseph is an excellent example of that reality. He is born into a complex, blended family where Jacob, his father, his two wives, two concubines and their children, all live under one roof. Joseph was Jacob's favored son. As a result, his brothers grew jealous, leading them to sell Joseph to a merchant who took him to Egypt. The brothers never expected to hear from Joseph again. After he is sold, Joseph's life becomes very difficult. For the next ten to thirteen years, Joseph lives first as a slave, and later, as a prisoner falsely accused of rape.

1. Imagine yourself in Joseph's shoes sitting in a prison cell without any hope of freedom. What thoughts, feelings, or doubts might you have about your family? About yourself? About God?

2. Through God's miraculous intervention, Joseph is pulled from the pit of prison and made the second most powerful person in Egypt. When his brothers come to him for help and food, Joseph invites them to bring their father and live in Egypt. After their father dies, the brothers begin to worry. Read Genesis. 50:15-21. What assumptions are the brothers making about Joseph?

........................................................................................................

........................................................................................................

........................................................................................................

........................................................................................................

........................................................................................................

3. Why do you think Joseph weeps (v.17)?[10]

........................................................................................................

........................................................................................................

........................................................................................................

........................................................................................................

4. Joseph chooses to break the "normal" way his family deals with hurt feelings and conflict by forgiving his brothers. How might you have responded if you were in Joseph's position? (Be sure to put yourself in Joseph's shoes).

........................................................................................................

........................................................................................................

........................................................................................................

........................................................................................................

........................................................................................................

5. Slowly, reread verses 19-21. Here we see Joseph's response to the enormous losses he experienced in his life. Carefully consider the different aspects of this response below. As you think about your own life story, which one speaks the most to you?

"Don't be afraid."

........................................................................................................

........................................................................................................

........................................................................................................

........................................................................................................

........................................................................................................

........................................................................................................

"Am I in the place of God?"

........................................................................................................

........................................................................................................

........................................................................................................

........................................................................................................

........................................................................................................

........................................................................................................

"You intended to harm me but God intended it for good…"

........................................................................................................

........................................................................................................

........................................................................................................

........................................................................................................

........................................................................................................

# GOING BACK IN ORDER TO
# GO FORWARD

## Applications/Exercises . . . . . . . . . . . . . . . . . . . .35 minutes
(10 minutes for chart and 25 minutes to answer questions 2-4)

Joseph had a rich sense of being part of his family of origin and how it had shaped his life.

1. Fill in the boxes below. You are encouraged to do this prayerfully, even if you have done a similar exercise before. We often receive new insights when we ponder and reflect on our family's impact on us at different times.[11]

- List the life messages you received from your parents or caretakers (e.g. Don't be weak. Education is everything. You must achieve to be loved. Don't be sad; things could be worse. Make a lot of money. Don't trust people; they will hurt you.)

- List any "earthquake" events that sent "aftershocks" into your extended family (e.g. abuse, premature or sudden deaths/losses, divorces, shameful secrets revealed, etc.)

- Look at the three separate boxes and summarize what messages about life/yourself/others you internalized. Then fill in the middle box, "Cumulative messages I received."

**Father (Caretaker)**     **Mother (Caretaker)**

Messages about life received:

Messages about life received:

"Earthquake" events in family history:

- 
- 
- 
- 
- 

Cumulative messages I received:

2. Share with the group the message(s) you received?

........................................................................................................

........................................................................................................

........................................................................................................

........................................................................................................

........................................................................................................

........................................................................................................

........................................................................................................

........................................................................................................

........................................................................................................

........................................................................................................

3. How do these messages compare with messages about who you are and how life is be lived in God's family?

........................................................................................................

........................................................................................................

........................................................................................................

........................................................................................................

........................................................................................................

........................................................................................................

........................................................................................................

........................................................................................................

........................................................................................................

........................................................................................................

4. What might be one specific message from your family that God is revealing to you today that you want to change as part of your "hard work of discipleship"?

.................................................................................................

.................................................................................................

.................................................................................................

.................................................................................................

.................................................................................................

.................................................................................................

.................................................................................................

.................................................................................................

5. Paul prays in Ephesians 1:18 that we might know his incomparably great power for us who believe. When we receive Jesus Christ, the person of the Holy Spirit comes to live inside of us. Pray for one another. Pray for yourself, asking God to transform you and that all of your life might be a blessing to others!

.................................................................................................

.................................................................................................

.................................................................................................

.................................................................................................

## For Next Week's Study

*Read Chapter 6, "Journey Through the Wall."*

## JOURNAL

# WEEK 4

## JOURNEY THROUGH

## THE WALL

## WEEK 4

### Journey Through the Wall
#### READING: CHAPTER 6

Emotionally healthy spirituality requires that you to go through the pain of the Wall—or, as the ancients called it, "the dark night of the soul." Just as a physical wall stops us from moving ahead, God sometimes stops us in our spiritual journey through a spiritual Wall in order to radically transform our character. Often, we are brought to the Wall by circumstances and crises beyond our control.

Regardless of how we get there, every follower of Jesus at some point will confront the Wall. Failure to understand and surrender to God's working in us at the Wall often results in great long-term pain, on-going immaturity and confusion. Receiving the gift of God in the Wall, however, transforms our lives forever.

## Growing Connected . . . . . . . . . . . . . . . . . . . . .10 minutes

1. In this season of your life, what is the greatest obstacle that you face? Explain.

........................................................................................

........................................................................................

........................................................................................

........................................................................................

........................................................................................

## Starters . . . . . . . . . . . . . . . . . . . . . . . . . . . . .15 minutes

*If using the DVD introduction, play it now.*

*(Read the following section only if you are not using the introduction from the DVD.)*

For most of us, the Wall appears through a crisis that turns our world upside down. It comes, perhaps, through a divorce, a job loss, the death of a close friend or family member, a cancer diagnosis, a disillusioning church experience, a betrayal, a shattered dream, a wayward child, a car accident, an inability to get pregnant, a deep desire to marry that remains unfulfilled, a spiritual dryness or a loss of joy in our relationship with God. We question ourselves, God, and the church. We discover for the first time that our faith does not appear to "work." We have more questions than answers as the very foundation of our faith feels like it is on the line. We don't know where God is, what he is doing, where he is going, how he is getting us there, or when this will be over…It (the Wall) is not simply a one-time event that we pass through and get beyond. It appears to be something we return to as part of our ongoing relationship with God (pp.120-121).

1. If you have been through a Wall, *briefly* share one way it impacted you and your view of God.[12]

**Bible Study — Genesis 22:1-14** . . . . . . . . . . . . . .**40 minutes**

Abraham, in his earthly pilgrimage with God, appears to go through a number of Walls. His greatest one, however, comes when God asks him to do the unthinkable — to kill his only son Isaac. Read Genesis 22:1-14.

1. How would you hear the words in verse 2: "Take your son, your only son, whom you love…sacrifice him?"

...........................................................................................................

...........................................................................................................

...........................................................................................................

...........................................................................................................

...........................................................................................................

...........................................................................................................

...........................................................................................................

2. What aspects of "the dark night" might be tormenting Abraham's soul as he bound his son Isaac and laid him on the altar? (e.g. weariness, sense of failure, defeat, emptiness, dryness, unbelief, guilt, disillusionment, abandonment by God).

...........................................................................................................

...........................................................................................................

...........................................................................................................

...........................................................................................................

...........................................................................................................

...........................................................................................................

3. In light of this story, how is your image of God challenged?

..................................................................................................

..................................................................................................

..................................................................................................

..................................................................................................

4. What are some possible reasons we have a hard time accepting and moving through Walls?[13]

..................................................................................................

..................................................................................................

..................................................................................................

..................................................................................................

5. Every believer, in order to grow in Christ, must go through Walls, or "dark nights of the soul." This is God's way of rewiring and "purging our affections and passions" that we might delight in his love and enter into a richer, fuller communion with him. In this way he frees us from unhealthy attachments and idolatries of the world. How might this larger perspective serve as an encouragement to you today?

..................................................................................................

..................................................................................................

..................................................................................................

..................................................................................................

6. In light of how the story ends, what do you learn about God as Provider (vs.14)?

..................................................................................................

..................................................................................................

..................................................................................................

## Applications/Exercises . . . . . . . . . . . . . . . . . . . .25 minutes
(5 minutes to journal and 20 minutes for sharing and prayer)

When God takes us through a Wall, we are changed. The following are four primary characteristics of life found on the other side of the Wall.

- Greater Level of Brokenness

- Greater Appreciation for Holy Unknowing (Mystery)

- A Deeper Ability to Wait on God

- A Greater Detachment (from the World)

Journaling can be a powerful tool to help clarify areas of our life where God desires to bring transformation. It illuminates what is going on inside of us. Few tools get us to the "issue beneath the issue" like journaling.

1. Choose one characteristic from the above list where you sense God is seeking to work in you now. Use the space provided here to journal your thoughts and feelings regarding how God is birthing something new in you and/or helping you shed incomplete or immature ideas about him.

........................................................................................................................

........................................................................................................................

........................................................................................................................

........................................................................................................................

........................................................................................................................

........................................................................................................................

........................................................................................................................

........................................................................................................................

........................................................................................................................

........................................................................................................................

.......................................................................................................

.......................................................................................................

.......................................................................................................

.......................................................................................................

.......................................................................................................

.......................................................................................................

.......................................................................................................

.......................................................................................................

.......................................................................................................

.......................................................................................................

2. End your time together in groups of two by sharing and praying for one another.

.......................................................................................................

.......................................................................................................

.......................................................................................................

.......................................................................................................

.......................................................................................................

## For Next Week's Study

*Read Chapter 7, "Enlarge Your Soul Through Grief and Loss."*

# WEEK 5
## ENLARGE YOUR SOUL
## THROUGH GRIEF AND LOSS

## WEEK 5

### Enlarge Your Soul Through Grief and Loss
#### READING: CHAPTER 7

Read the following paragraphs slowly and thoughtfully.

Loss is a place where self-knowledge and powerful transformation can happen—if we have the courage to participate fully in the process.

We all face many "deaths" within our lives. Our culture routinely interprets these losses and griefs as alien invasions and interruptions to our "normal" lives. The choice is whether these deaths will be terminal (crushing our spirit and life) or will open us up to new possibilities and depths of transformation in Christ.

# ENLARGE YOUR SOUL THROUGH GRIEF AND LOSS

## Growing Connected . . . . . . . . . . . . . . . . . . . . . .10 minutes

1. As you were growing up, how did you deal with your disappointments? Give one example.

.............................................................................................

.............................................................................................

.............................................................................................

.............................................................................................

## Starters . . . . . . . . . . . . . . . . . . . . . . . . . . . . .15 minutes

*If using the DVD introduction, play it now.*

1. Briefly share one loss you have experienced this past year. How has this loss impacted you?

.............................................................................................

.............................................................................................

.............................................................................................

.............................................................................................

.............................................................................................

.............................................................................................

.............................................................................................

.............................................................................................

.............................................................................................

.............................................................................................

.............................................................................................

## Bible Study — Matthew 26:31–44 ...........35 minutes

The end of Jesus' vibrant, popular, earthly life and ministry appeared to be an enormous loss to his disciples and followers. In this passage we will observe two very different approaches to that loss — the apostle Peter and Jesus. Read Matthew 26:31–44.

1. Peter was deeply invested in Jesus and his kingdom, having left everything to follow him. What is Peter's response to Jesus' shocking prediction (vv.31-36)?

.......................................................................................................

.......................................................................................................

.......................................................................................................

2. Below is a list of common defenses we often use to protect ourselves from grief and loss. Circle the common defenses Peter uses to protect himself against the painful reality of Jesus' prediction:

- Denial

- Minimizing (admitting something is wrong, but in such a way that it appears less serious than it actually is)

- Blaming others (or God)

- "Over-spiritualizing"

- Blaming himself

- Rationalizing (offering excuses and justifications)

- Intellectualizing (giving analysis and theories to avoid personal awareness or difficult feelings)

- Distracting

- Becoming hostile

- Medicating (with unhealthy addictions or attachments to numb our pain)

3. Based on the list above, can you name defenses you tend to use when dealing with loss and setbacks, and why?

......................................................................................................

......................................................................................................

......................................................................................................

......................................................................................................

......................................................................................................

......................................................................................................

......................................................................................................

......................................................................................................

......................................................................................................

......................................................................................................

......................................................................................................

......................................................................................................

......................................................................................................

......................................................................................................

......................................................................................................

......................................................................................................

......................................................................................................

......................................................................................................

......................................................................................................

......................................................................................................

......................................................................................................

......................................................................................................

4. It is important for us to remember that Jesus was both fully human and fully God. Spend a few moments looking at Jesus in vv.36–41. In contrast to the list above, what are some of the ways he deals with and moves through his losses?[14]

........................................................................................................

........................................................................................................

........................................................................................................

........................................................................................................

........................................................................................................

........................................................................................................

........................................................................................................

........................................................................................................

........................................................................................................

........................................................................................................

5. What about Jesus' example of grieving most speaks to you about embracing your own grief and loss?

........................................................................................................

........................................................................................................

........................................................................................................

........................................................................................................

........................................................................................................

........................................................................................................

........................................................................................................

........................................................................................................

# ENLARGE YOUR SOUL THROUGH GRIEF AND LOSS

## Applications/Exercises . . . . . . . . . . . . . . . . . . . .30 minutes

(Take 10 minutes to journal questions 1 and 2)

  1. Using the chart below, choose two or three age ranges, and write down your significant losses during those years.

| GRIEF CHART | | |
|---|---|---|
| Age (in years) | Losses/Disappointments Experienced | Your Response at that Time |
| 3–12 | | |
| 13–18 | | |
| 19–25 | | |
| 25–40 | | |
| 40 & older | | |

2. What was the experience of filling out the chart like for you? Did it reveal anything new to you? Explain.

....................................................................................................................

....................................................................................................................

....................................................................................................................

....................................................................................................................

....................................................................................................................

....................................................................................................................

....................................................................................................................

....................................................................................................................

....................................................................................................................

....................................................................................................................

....................................................................................................................

....................................................................................................................

....................................................................................................................

....................................................................................................................

....................................................................................................................

....................................................................................................................

....................................................................................................................

....................................................................................................................

....................................................................................................................

....................................................................................................................

3. One of the central messages of Christianity is that suffering and death bring resurrection and new life. Are there any losses you have not yet embraced where new life is still waiting to be birthed?[15]

.........................................................................................................

.........................................................................................................

.........................................................................................................

.........................................................................................................

.........................................................................................................

.........................................................................................................

.........................................................................................................

.........................................................................................................

.........................................................................................................

.........................................................................................................

.........................................................................................................

.........................................................................................................

.........................................................................................................

4. Pray together as a group regarding what is in your heart in response to this study.

.........................................................................................................

.........................................................................................................

.........................................................................................................

## For Next Week's Study

*Read Chapter 8, "Discover the Rhythms of the Daily Office and Sabbath."*

## JOURNAL

# WEEK 6
## DISCOVER THE RHYTHMS
## OF THE DAILY OFFICE
## AND SABBATH

## WEEK 6

### Discover the Rhythms of the Daily Office and Sabbath
#### READING: CHAPTER 8

Many of us are eager to develop our relationship with God. The problem, however, is that we can't seem to stop long enough to be *with* him. And if we aren't busy, we feel guilty that we are wasting time and not being productive. It is like being addicted — not to drugs or alcohol — but to tasks, work and doing.

But God *is* offering us a way to deeply root our lives in him. This can be found in two ancient disciplines going back thousands of years — the Daily Office and Sabbath. When placed inside present-day Christianity, the Daily Office and Sabbath are groundbreaking, counter-cultural acts that go against the grain of our fast-paced Western culture.

Stopping for the Daily Office and Sabbath is not meant to add another "to-do" to our already busy schedules. It is the resetting of our entire lives toward a new destination — God himself. These practices enable us to stay attuned to God's presence throughout our days and weeks.

## Growing Connected . . . . . . . . . . . . . . . . . . . . . .10 minutes

1. What is one practice you do on a daily/weekly basis that helps you stay connected to God?[16]

........................................................................................................

........................................................................................................

........................................................................................................

........................................................................................................

## Starters . . . . . . . . . . . . . . . . . . . . . . . . . . . . . .20 minutes

*If using the DVD introduction, play it now.*

We now have the opportunity to experience this practice called the Daily Office.

1. Choose one person to read the following guidelines for the Daily Office aloud.

- For the next ten minutes, we are going to engage in what is called a Daily Office. An Office is a time to *stop, slow down, center,* and *pause* to be with Jesus.

- Notice there is silence for one minute at the beginning and conclusion of each Office.

- We will also pause for about fifteen seconds *between* the readings/prayers.

- Take a minute and get an overview of the Scriptures we will be praying together. We will pray them aloud together. Watch for the facilitator's cue.

# DISCOVER THE RHYTHMS OF THE DAILY OFFICE AND SABBATH

## DAILY OFFICE

**Facilitator:** "To begin, I invite you to close your eyes for a few moments: Step out of all your roles in life –e.g. father, mother, leader, employee, boss, student, friend, brother, sister, teacher. Right now, you are only a child of God. To prepare for this Daily Office, imagine God delighting in you as a parent delights in their child. He is eager to give you his undivided attention, his time. His eyes sparkle as he gazes upon your face. He is smiling and loving all over you. What are the words you would love to hear God say to you? Allow him to speak those words over you."[17]

"As Scripture instructs us to '*Be still and know that I am God*' (Psalm 46:10 NRSV), we will begin and end our time together with 1 minute of silence."

### SILENCE (1 MINUTE)

### OPENING PRAYER

**Facilitator:** "Let's read aloud together"

> **Together:**
>
> *Teach us to number our days aright,*
>
> > *that we may gain a heart of wisdom.*
>
> *For a thousand years in your sight*
>
> > *are like a day that has just gone by*
> >
> > *or like a watch in the night.*
>
> *May the favor of the Lord our God rest upon us;*
>
> > *establish the work of our hands for us —*
> >
> > *yes, establish the work of our hands.*
>
> > > (Psalm 90: 4, 12, 17)

## PAUSE (15 SECONDS)

**Facilitator:** "Let's read aloud together"

**Together:**

> *We wait in hope for the LORD;*
>
> > *he is our help and our shield.*
>
> *In him our hearts rejoice,*
>
> > *for we trust in his holy name.*
>
> *May your unfailing love rest upon us,*
>
> > *O LORD,*
>
> > *even as we put our hope in you.*

(Psalm 33:20-22 NIV)

## PAUSE (15 SECONDS)

**Facilitator:** "Let's read aloud together"

**Together:**

> *'Our Father who is in heaven,*
>
> *Hallowed be Your name.*
>
> *'Your kingdom come.*
>
> *Your will be done,*
>
> > *On earth as it is in heaven.*
>
> *'Give us this day our daily bread.*
>
> *And forgive us our debts,*
>
> > *as we also have forgiven our debtors.*
>
> *And do not lead us into temptation,*
>
> > *but deliver us from evil.*
>
> *For Yours is the kingdom and the power and the glory forever. Amen.*

(Matthew 6:9-14 NASB95)

## Pause (15 seconds)

## Concluding Prayer

**Facilitator:** "Let's read aloud together"

**Together:**

> Lord, you say that *"in repentance and rest is your salvation, in quiet-ness and trust is your strength."* Teach me to rest and trust in you throughout the remainder of this day. *"Teach me your way, O LORD, and I will walk in your truth; give me an undivided heart that I may fear your name. . . For great is your love toward me."*
>
> (Isaiah 30:15b NIV and Psalm 86:11, 13a NIV)

## Conclude with Silence (1 minute)

CB BO

1. In the group, briefly share your thoughts and feelings about this experience.[18]

...........................................................................................................

...........................................................................................................

...........................................................................................................

...........................................................................................................

...........................................................................................................

...........................................................................................................

...........................................................................................................

...........................................................................................................

...........................................................................................................

...........................................................................................................

...........................................................................................................

# DISCOVER THE RHYTHMS OF THE DAILY OFFICE AND SABBATH

## Bible Study — Daniel 6:6–10; Exodus 20 . . . . . .40 minutes

After being forcibly removed from his country and home, Daniel was given a prestigious education and high-level job in government. The pressure on him to conform to the worldly, pagan values of Babylon was great. The following example gives us insight into one of the secrets of his faithful devotion to God. Read Daniel 6:6-10.

1. Reread verse 10 aloud. How do the words in this verse speak to you?

......................................................................................................

......................................................................................................

......................................................................................................

......................................................................................................

......................................................................................................

......................................................................................................

2. How do you think this practice anchored Daniel in God and enabled him to resist the great pressure he was facing?[19]

......................................................................................................

......................................................................................................

......................................................................................................

......................................................................................................

......................................................................................................

......................................................................................................

......................................................................................................

3. What costs were involved for Daniel?

......................................................................................................

......................................................................................................

......................................................................................................

......................................................................................................

......................................................................................................

......................................................................................................

......................................................................................................

......................................................................................................

......................................................................................................

4. What are the greatest obstacles preventing you from stopping to be with God two or three times a day?

......................................................................................................

......................................................................................................

......................................................................................................

......................................................................................................

......................................................................................................

......................................................................................................

......................................................................................................

......................................................................................................

......................................................................................................

5. These are the Ten Commandments. Review the Fourth Commandment found in Exodus 20:8-11.

*1st — You shall have no other gods before me.*

*2nd — You shall not make for yourself an idol.*

*3rd — You shall not misuse the name of the LORD your God.*

*4th — Remember the Sabbath day by keeping it holy. Six days you shall labor and do all your work, but the seventh day is a Sabbath to the LORD your God. On it you shall not do any work, neither you, nor your son or daughter, nor your manservant or maidservant, nor your animals, nor the alien within your gates. For in six days the LORD made the heavens and the earth, the sea and all that is in them, but he rested on the seventh day. Therefore the LORD blessed the Sabbath day and made it holy.*

*5th — Honor your father and your mother.*

*6th — You shall not murder.*

*7th — You shall not commit adultery.*

*8th — You shall not steal.*

*9th — You shall not give false testimony.*

*10th — You shall not covet.*

(Exodus 20:1-17)

Sabbath is engaging in a regular rhythm of stopping, resting, delighting and contemplating God for a twenty-four hour block of time each week.

What, if any, is your current practice around Sabbath keeping?

............................................................................................................

............................................................................................................

............................................................................................................

............................................................................................................

............................................................................................................

## Applications/Exercises . . . . . . . . . . . . . . . . . . . .20 minutes

Biblical Sabbaths have four foundational qualities that distinguish them from a "day off."

- **Stop** — "To stop" is built into the literal meaning of the Hebrew word. We have limits. God is on the throne running the world. We are called to let go and trust him.

- **Rest** — Once we stop, we are called to rest from our work and our "doings."

- **Delight** — We are to slow down so we can enjoy what we have been given.

- **Contemplate** — We are to ponder the love of God. Every Sabbath we taste the glorious eternal party that awaits us when we see him face to face (see Revelation 22:4)

Sabbath is like receiving the gift of a heavy snow day every week. Stores are closed. Roads are impassable. Suddenly you have the gift of a day to do whatever you want. You don't have any obligations, pressures, or responsibilities. You have permission to play, be with friends, take a nap, read a good book. Few of us would give ourselves a "no obligation day" very often. God does—every seventh day.

Think about it. He gives you over seven weeks a year (fifty-two days in all) of snow days every year![20]

**Read question 1 and 2. Briefly share from one of them.**

1. What difference would it make in your life if you celebrated a Sabbath every week?

....................................................................................................

....................................................................................................

....................................................................................................

....................................................................................................

....................................................................................................

2. What questions, concerns or fears do you have that keep you from making this practice a part of your weekly rhythm?

..................................................................................................................

..................................................................................................................

..................................................................................................................

..................................................................................................................

..................................................................................................................

..................................................................................................................

..................................................................................................................

..................................................................................................................

3. Journal a Response: Both the Daily Office and the Sabbath are concerned with a rhythm in our days and our weeks. In the space provided below, take 2-3 minutes to journal one small step you can take to begin to incorporate one of these two ancient disciplines?

..................................................................................................................

..................................................................................................................

..................................................................................................................

..................................................................................................................

..................................................................................................................

**Close in prayer together, committing your plan to God.**

## For Next Week's Study

*Read Chapter 9, "Grow into an Emotionally Mature Adult."*

## JOURNAL

....................................................................................................................

....................................................................................................................

....................................................................................................................

....................................................................................................................

....................................................................................................................

....................................................................................................................

....................................................................................................................

....................................................................................................................

....................................................................................................................

....................................................................................................................

....................................................................................................................

....................................................................................................................

....................................................................................................................

....................................................................................................................

....................................................................................................................

....................................................................................................................

....................................................................................................................

....................................................................................................................

....................................................................................................................

....................................................................................................................

....................................................................................................................

....................................................................................................................

# WEEK 7

## GROW INTO
## AN EMOTIONALLY
## MATURE ADULT

# WEEK 7

## Grow into an Emotionally Mature Adult

### READING: CHAPTER 9

The goal of the Christian life is to love well. Jesus was aware that true spirituality included not only loving God, but also the skill of loving others maturely.

Growing into an emotionally mature Christian person includes experiencing each individual, including myself, as sacred, or as Martin Buber put it, as a "Thou" rather than an "It". Becoming emotionally mature requires learning, practicing and integrating such skills as speaking respectfully, listening with empathy, negotiating conflict fairly and uncovering the hidden expectations I have of others...just to name a few.

As we will see in today's Bible study on the parable of the Good Samaritan, both self-respect and compassion for others are part of a life rooted in "I-Thou" relating.

# GROW INTO AN EMOTIONALLY MATURE ADULT

## Growing Connected . . . . . . . . . . . . . . . . . . . . .10 minutes

1. Brainstorm and jot down qualities that describe emotional immaturity and emotional maturity in the circles below. As you think about these qualities, consider how we treat/view ourselves and how we treat/view other people.

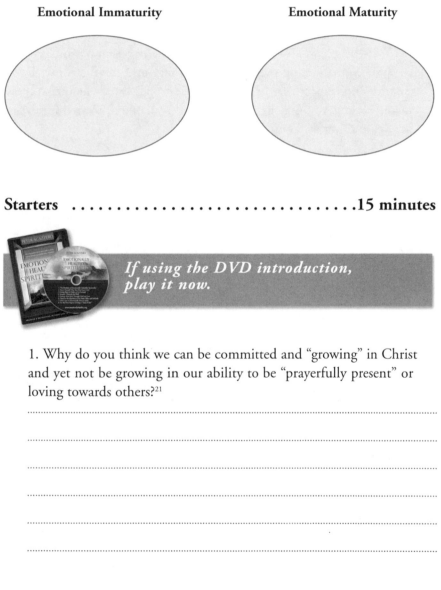

**Emotional Immaturity**

**Emotional Maturity**

## Starters . . . . . . . . . . . . . . . . . . . . . . . . . . . . .15 minutes

*If using the DVD introduction, play it now.*

1. Why do you think we can be committed and "growing" in Christ and yet not be growing in our ability to be "prayerfully present" or loving towards others?[21]

........................................................................

........................................................................

........................................................................

........................................................................

........................................................................

........................................................................

# GROW INTO AN EMOTIONALLY MATURE ADULT

## Bible Study — Luke 10:25–37 . . . . . . . . . . . . .35 minutes

Who can hear a story on the news about someone getting mugged, robbed, stripped naked and left for dead in an alleyway without being affected? These real life stories also happened in the days of Jesus. Today's passage is also a very disturbing story. Read Luke 10:25–37.

1. According to Martin Buber,[22] the great Jewish theologian, we treat people as an "It" when we use them as means to an end or as objects. We treat people as a "Thou," when we recognize each person as a separate human being made in God's image and treat them with dignity and respect. If you were the priest or Levite, what are some of the reasons you may have passed by this man and treated him as an "It" and not a "Thou"?

.............................................................................................................

.............................................................................................................

.............................................................................................................

.............................................................................................................

.............................................................................................................

.............................................................................................................

2. Looking at vv. 31-33, what did the Samaritan see and feel that the priest and Levite did not?

.............................................................................................................

.............................................................................................................

.............................................................................................................

.............................................................................................................

.............................................................................................................

3. Journal your thoughts on the following questions for two minutes:

a. Can you think of a time when you were seen in a negative light, or treated as inferior, or passed over as invisible? How did it feel?

.................................................................................................................

.................................................................................................................

.................................................................................................................

.................................................................................................................

.................................................................................................................

.................................................................................................................

.................................................................................................................

.................................................................................................................

b. Who have you been taught not to see or to treat as an "It"?

.................................................................................................................

.................................................................................................................

.................................................................................................................

.................................................................................................................

.................................................................................................................

.................................................................................................................

.................................................................................................................

.................................................................................................................

4. Would one or two of you be willing to share your responses from the above questions?

5. Reread verses 33-36. The Samaritan's compassion leads him to stop and to help the hurting man. At the same time, how does he demonstrate self-respect and awareness of his limits?

.......................................................................................................................

.......................................................................................................................

.......................................................................................................................

.......................................................................................................................

.......................................................................................................................

6. What are some of your challenges when it comes to loving your neighbor and loving yourself?[23]

.......................................................................................................................

.......................................................................................................................

.......................................................................................................................

.......................................................................................................................

.......................................................................................................................

7. In light of how God is coming to you through this study, how do you hear the words in v. 37 to "go and do likewise"?

.......................................................................................................................

.......................................................................................................................

.......................................................................................................................

.......................................................................................................................

.......................................................................................................................

# Grow into an Emotionally Mature Adult

## Applications/Exercises . . . . . . . . . . . . . . . . . . . .30 minutes

One way of growing in the area of loving others well, *and treating ourselves and others as a "Thou"*, is to understand how we manage our **expectations** in relationships.[24]

EXPECTATIONS are ASSUMPTIONS about what someone SHOULD do. Every time I make an assumption about someone without checking it out, it is likely I am treating them as an "It" and not a "Thou." Why? I am jumping to conclusions without having checked out the assumption. Consider how you feel when someone is angry with you because you didn't fulfill their expectations, yet they never communicated this to you. They simply assumed you should know.

Unmet and unclear expectations can create havoc in our places of employment, classrooms, friendships, dating relationships, marriages, sports teams, families, and churches. We expect other people to know what we want before we say it. The problem with most expectations is that they are:

- **unconscious** — we may have expectations we're not even aware of until we are disappointed by someone

- **unrealistic** — we may develop unrealistic expectations by watching TV, movies, or other people/resources that give false impressions

- **unspoken** — we may have never told our spouse, friend, or employee what we expect, yet we are angry when our "expectations" are not met

- **un-agreed upon** — we may have had our own thoughts about what was expected that were never agreed upon by the other person

# Grow into an Emotionally Mature Adult

1. Think of a recent, simple expectation that went unmet and made you angry or disappointed.[25] For example: I expected my husband to accompany me to my office party this past weekend. I expected to socialize with members of my small group outside the meeting times. I expected my teenager to put their dirty dishes in the dishwasher. I expected my boss to give me at least a 5% cost of living raise last year.

Write yours down.

........................................................................................

........................................................................................

........................................................................................

........................................................................................

........................................................................................

........................................................................................

........................................................................................

........................................................................................

2. Compare them with the inventory questions below:

- **conscious** — Were you conscious (aware) you had this expectation?

- **realistic** — Is the expectation realistic regarding the other person?

- **spoken** — Have you clearly spoken the expectation to them or do you just think "they should know"?

- **agreed upon** — Has the other person agreed to the expectation?

**Remember this principle:** *Expectations are only valid when they have been mutually agreed upon.* These are the expectations we have a right to expect.

3. Break into groups of two or three and respond to the following two questions:

- What did you discover about your expectations?

........................................................................................................................

........................................................................................................................

........................................................................................................................

........................................................................................................................

........................................................................................................................

........................................................................................................................

- What step(s) can you take to make the expectation conscious, spoken, realistic, and agreed upon so that you are relating in an "I-Thou" way?

........................................................................................................................

........................................................................................................................

........................................................................................................................

........................................................................................................................

........................................................................................................................

4. Pray. Ask God to grant you the courage to make the changes you need in the way you relate to others; i.e., to love maturely by treating yourself and others as a "Thou" rather than an "It."

## For Next Week's Study

**Read Chapter 10, "Go the Next Step to Develop a 'Rule of Life.'"**

## JOURNAL

........................................................................................

........................................................................................

........................................................................................

........................................................................................

........................................................................................

........................................................................................

........................................................................................

........................................................................................

........................................................................................

........................................................................................

........................................................................................

........................................................................................

........................................................................................

........................................................................................

........................................................................................

........................................................................................

........................................................................................

........................................................................................

........................................................................................

........................................................................................

........................................................................................

........................................................................................

# Week 8
## Go the Next Step
## to Develop a
## "Rule of Life"

# WEEK 8

## Go the Next Step to Develop a "Rule of Life"
### READING: CHAPTER 10

If we are to nurture a heart that treats people, and ourselves, as "Thou's" instead of "It's", we need to be intentional about our lives. By ordering our lives to contemplate the love of Christ and to receive the love of Christ, we will be able to give the love of Christ away to others. In this way, he transforms our lives into a gift to our families, friends, coworkers, and communities.

The problem again, however, is our busyness and lack of intentionality. Often, we find ourselves unfocused, distracted, and spiritually adrift. Few of us have a conscious plan for intentionally developing our spiritual lives.

Nurturing a growing spirituality in our present-day culture calls for a thoughtful, conscious, purposeful plan. To do this well, however, requires us to uncover another ancient buried treasure — a "Rule of Life."

# Go the Next Step to Develop a "Rule of Life"

## Growing Connected . . . . . . . . . . . . . . . . . . . . . .10 minutes

1. Before we launch into our final study, it is important that we pause and consider the past seven studies:

- The Problem of Emotionally Unhealthy Spirituality
  (Saul — emotionally unaware and not cultivating his relationship with God)

- Know Yourself that You May Know God
  (David — courageously living out of his true self)

- Going Back in Order to Go Forward
  (Joseph — transformed by a very difficult past)

- Journey Through the Wall
  (Abraham — trusting God in a "dark night of the soul")

- Enlarge Your Soul Through Grief and Loss
  (Jesus in Gethsemane — embracing God's will)

- Discover the Rhythms of the Daily Office and Sabbath
  (Daniel — anchoring himself in God)

- Grow into an Emotionally Mature Adult
  (The Good Samaritan — modeling an "I-Thou" heart to others)

In light of how God has been coming to you throughout these studies, complete the following sentence:

I am beginning to realize…

.................................................................................................................

.................................................................................................................

.................................................................................................................

# Go the Next Step to Develop a "Rule of Life"

**Starters** . . . . . . . . . . . . . . . . . . . . . . . . . . . . . . . . . .15 minutes

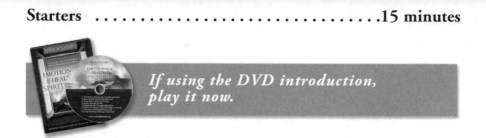

*If using the DVD introduction, play it now.*

1. Think about your life in terms of prayer, rest, work/activity and relationships. In each box, write one specific thing you are currently doing in each of these four areas to nurture your relationship with Jesus.

| Prayer | Rest |
|---|---|
| | |
| **Work/Activity** | **Relationships** |
| | |

# Go the Next Step to Develop a "Rule of Life"

## Bible Study — Acts 2:42–47 . . . . . . . . . . . . . . .15 minutes[26]

The Rule of Life will be introduced to us as we study the first Christian community.

The word Rule comes from the Greek for "trellis." A trellis is a tool that enables a grapevine to get off the ground and grow upward, becoming more fruitful and productive. In the same way, a Rule of Life is a trellis that helps us abide in Christ and become more fruitful spiritually.[27]

1. In the book of Acts, we are given a window into the life of the first community of believers soon after the coming of the Holy Spirit at Pentecost. Three thousand people have just come to faith in Christ. Read Acts 2:42-47. What speaks to you from this passage?

..............................................................................................................

..............................................................................................................

..............................................................................................................

..............................................................................................................

..............................................................................................................

2. Based on this one passage, how would you describe their Rule of Life? Describe the activities/disciplines they use to grow and mature in Christ.[28]

..............................................................................................................

..............................................................................................................

..............................................................................................................

..............................................................................................................

..............................................................................................................

..............................................................................................................

# GO THE NEXT STEP TO DEVELOP A "RULE OF LIFE"

**Applications/Exercises** .................... **.50 minutes**
(Take 5 minutes to slowly read this introduction.)

Now it is time for you to begin developing your own personal Rule of Life. The following story and questions are meant to help you discern what may be getting in the way of developing a way of life that keeps you closely connected to God.

In his book *A Hidden Wholeness,* Parker Palmer relates a story about farmers in the Midwest who would prepare for blizzards by tying a rope from the back door of their house out to the barn as a guide to ensure they could return safely home. These blizzards came quickly and fiercely and were highly dangerous. When their full force was blowing, a farmer could not see the end of his or her hand. Many froze to death in those blizzards, disoriented by their inability to see. They wandered in circles, lost sometimes in their own backyards. If they lost their grip on the rope, it became impossible for them to find their way home. Some froze within feet of their own front door, never realizing how close they were to safety.

Many of us are wandering amidst the blizzards of life and have lost our way spiritually.

1. Take fifteen minutes for time alone with God around the following questions:[29]

• What is the nature of your blizzard at this time?

.............................................................................

.............................................................................

.............................................................................

.............................................................................

.............................................................................

.............................................................................

.............................................................................

.............................................................................

.............................................................................

# GO THE NEXT STEP TO DEVELOP A "RULE OF LIFE"

• What contributes to your blizzard? What does it look like?
Feel like?

........................................................................................................

........................................................................................................

........................................................................................................

........................................................................................................

........................................................................................................

........................................................................................................

........................................................................................................

........................................................................................................

........................................................................................................

........................................................................................................

........................................................................................................

• What does that blizzard obscure? What gets "lost"?

........................................................................................................

........................................................................................................

........................................................................................................

........................................................................................................

........................................................................................................

........................................................................................................

........................................................................................................

........................................................................................................

........................................................................................................

........................................................................................................

# Go the Next Step to Develop a
# "Rule of Life"

- We each need a rope to keep us connected to God. Notice that every rope is actually made up of a series of smaller, intertwined threads. In light of your life at this time, what "threads" do you want to make up your rope (Rule of Life)?

..............................................................................................

..............................................................................................

..............................................................................................

..............................................................................................

..............................................................................................

..............................................................................................

..............................................................................................

..............................................................................................

..............................................................................................

..............................................................................................

..............................................................................................

2. After your time alone, get into groups of two. Share what you discovered in your time alone. (10 minutes)

3. Gather as a large group and invite those who would like to share how God is coming to them regarding the blizzard and their own personal "Rule of Life"? (10 minutes)

4. As a group, spend time in prayer, giving thanks to God for your time both in the group and for the new things God is doing in your journey with him. (10 minutes)

CR BO

# GENERAL
# LEADER'S NOTES

1. Read the introduction provided at the beginning of each study aloud to the group even if you are using the DVD. This will create a context for launching into the study.

2. We strongly suggest you use the DVD introductions for your group. If you do, however, there will only be time for one or two responses to the Starter question. The Starter question helps to launch the session, but don't linger here. It is important that you move forward into the heart of the study.

3. The nature of this material easily lends itself to lengthy sharing. One of your greatest challenges as the group leader/facilitator will be to keep the group focused and to share within the time frames allotted for each part of the study. It is important to cover each section of every study in order to give your group broad exposure to each topic as they Begin the Journey into Emotionally Healthy Spirituality.

4. If your group is large, you may want to break into smaller groups of three to four people so that everyone has a chance to participate.

5. When appropriate, it would be helpful for you to lead by being vulnerable and open with your own journey with this material.

6. Remember, we are only experts on our own journey. Respect where each person is in their journey with Christ. The Holy Spirit will prompt and lead each person differently at different times through this material. Remember that people change slowly — including yourself.

## Additional Suggestions from *Leading Bible Discussions* (InterVarsity).

1. Avoid answering your own questions. Feel free to rephrase a question until it is clearly understood.

2. Encourage more than one answer to each question. Ask, "What do the rest of you think?" or "Anyone else?"

3. Try to be affirming whenever possible. Let people know you appreciate their contributions.

4. Try not to reject an answer. If it is clearly wrong, ask, "What in the passage led you to that conclusion?"

5. Avoid going off on tangents. If people wander off course, gently bring them back to the subject at hand.

CR ഓ

# LEADER'S NOTES FOR
# EACH STUDY

# Leader's Notes for Each Study

## Week 1: The Problem of Emotionally Unhealthy Spirituality

If this is your small group's first meeting, you will need to add an extra half hour to this first study in order to get acquainted and cover the "housekeeping" points outlined below. This will need to be done before you begin the study itself.

Be sure to cover the following details for your first meeting:

- Have name tags, Bibles, *Emotionally Healthy Spirituality Workbooks*, *Emotionally Healthy Spirituality* books and pens for those who don't have them. If you are using the DVDs be sure to set up ahead of time so you are ready to go.

- Be ready 15 minutes early.

- Greet and welcome each person individually.

- Review the dates and time the group will be meeting.

[1]The leader/facilitator will want to read and be familiar with other examples from Chapter 2 on the "10 Top Symptoms of Emotionally Unhealthy Spirituality, Ibid. pp. 23.

[2]The command to "totally destroy everything," including women and children, presents a difficult moral and theological problem for the modern reader. Shortly after leaving Egypt, the Israelites "weary and worn out" were attacked by the Amalekites (Exodus 17:8-16). After God granted his people victory, he promised to completely destroy the Amalekites from the face of the earth (see also Deuteronomy 25:17-18). Now, through Saul, God determines to carry out his threat. You may want to mention three reasons for such a command. First, Israel was functioning as an instrument of God's judgment on a wicked, utterly sinful culture. Second, Israel needed to eliminate all forms of temptation that might corrupt and prevent them from being God's chosen instrument in the world. This drastic action was needed to maintain holiness (Deuteronomy 7:1-6, 20:16-18). Finally, in Hebrew the phrase "totally destroy" means "to devote to Yahweh." The spoils, then, were surrendered and dedicated to God and were in some way a sacrifice to God. Be careful not to spend much time on this point.

[3]For those who have not read the book, you will want to explain the iceberg illustration found on pages 15, 16 of Chapter 1 of *Emotionally Healthy Spirituality*.

[4]See page 45 and 46 from *Emotionally Healthy Spirituality* (Nelson, 2006) for a full description of contemplative spirituality and emotional health.

## Week 2: Know Yourself that You May Know God

[5]Before you begin this study:

- Take a few minutes to warmly welcome each member.

- Introduce the topic, by mentioning that in the last study, the group looked at Saul and the problem of emotionally unhealthy spirituality. But this week, we will look at David and the first principle of emotionally healthy spirituality — Knowing Yourself that You May Know God.

- Reread aloud the guidelines from page 7 for your time together as a small group.

[6]When people share about their dream job, be aware that it can, very often, give you (and them) a glimpse of their "true self" in surprising ways.

[7]You may want to reread the section on "Discovering God's Will and Your Emotions" from page 73-74 from *Emotionally Healthy Spirituality* (Nelson, 2006) for a brief summary on the role of feelings in discerning God's will.

[8]This exercise may bring up significant pain in some of the members of the group. (e.g. unresolved anger, sadness that has not been grieved, shame that has been masked). Remember that this is a limited exercise with one goal — to help people begin to be aware of how much is going on inside of them. This is not the time to fix or give advice. Giving people space to express their feelings is a gift enough. If "pandora's box" opens for a member of the group, thank the person for their awareness and vulnerability. Let them know that, if they would like, you will be glad to talk with them after the group. It is important to recognize your role as facilitator/small group leader and not a professional counselor. In some cases, you may want to direct them to get the help they need beyond the limits of your group.

[9]One very helpful way to clarify this process of growing into our true selves in a new way is through use of a new term: differentiation. It refers to a person's capacity to "define his or her own life's goals and values apart from the pressures of those around them." The key emphasis of differentiation is on the ability to think clearly and carefully as another means, besides our feelings, of knowing ourselves.

It involves the ability to hold on to who you are and who you are not. The degree to which you are able to affirm your distinct values and goals apart from the pressures around you (separateness) while remaining close to people important to you (togetherness) helps determine your level of differentiation. People, like David, who are highly differentiated, can choose how they want to be without being controlled by the approval or disapproval of others. Intensity of feelings, high stress, or the anxiety of others around them does not overwhelm their capacity to think intelligently.

## Week 3: Going Back In Order to Go Forward

[10]There is no way we can know for sure why Joseph weeps but numerous possibilities exist. Perhaps he weeps because once again he realizes they are lying. Maybe he knows Jacob never left instructions that he should not harm them. Maybe he realizes his brothers will never really change; they are still lying. Or it could be that they are finally admitting their terrible cruelty and sins against Joseph. And Joseph is weeping because his pain is finally validated or acknowledged. It could be that these are tears of joy as he realizes this is the fulfillment of his dream from Genesis 37, or that all the pain of his life has led to the truth of this moment where he must make a momentous decision of whether or not to forgive.

[11]Encourage those who may have done work on their family of origin in some other setting, or even filled out the chart prior to the group meeting, to prayerfully ponder this exercise again. God often surprises us with fresh insights when we have space to contemplate these messages before him.

## Week 4 Journey Through the Wall

[12]It usually takes time to share about a Wall in a person's life. In light of only having fifteen minutes for this starter section, you as a leader/facilitator may want to take this time to share about a Wall you have experienced. We found that a well-thought out testimony can sometimes be better than open sharing at this point. Stories about Walls can be very long! At the very least, only one or two people will have time to share.

[13]We often carry within us inaccurate beliefs, or ideas, about God. For example, we take, "Delight yourself in the Lord and he will give you the desires of your heart" (Psalm 37:4) to mean that if we are doing all we think God wants, then only good things will follow. The problem is that this contradicts other Scriptures such as our text here. Abraham was, as far

as Scripture indicates, doing God's will. Yet it surely was not the desire of Abraham's heart to kill his son! Job is another classic example. He is an innocent sufferer. What makes his life so bewildering is the undeserved nature of his pain. The principle that we reap what we sow (Galatians 6:7-8) did not apply to Job as his friends argued in Job 3-37. For this reason, embracing our Walls frequently results in a crisis of faith for many believers rather than a doorway to transformation.

## Week 5: Enlarge Your Soul Through Grief and Loss

[14]Jesus' response to his grief and loss stands in sharp contrast to Peter. Jesus, for example, feels deeply his sorrow and pain. He does not "spin" or spiritualize it away. Jesus openly admits his grief to those close to him and asks for their support. He repeatedly prays to his Father for an alternative, but finally accepts the Father's "no". We see him move through a process from struggling to accept the Father's will to finally rising up to embrace it.

[15]Two questions frequently come up in relation to grieving.

### 1. How do I know I am grieving or if I should be grieving?

One way to know if we are grieving is when we experience some of the following symptoms that normally accompany the stages of grieving — depression, anger, disbelief, yearning, bargaining, disbelief. On the other hand, if you go through a significant loss but do not experience any of the above feelings, you may need a mature, objective outsider to help you move through the process.

### 2. How do I know when I am done grieving?

There are many factors that impact the amount of time needed. For example, the deeper the loss, the more time needed to grieve. The loss felt when a child leaves home and goes off to college is very different than the loss experienced should that child die tragically. Another factor is to respect how God has crafted each of us differently. The time you need and I need may be very different. One key principle is to not censor your emotions that come bubbling up as a result of the loss. Allow yourself, like Jesus and David, to feel them deeply before God. Censoring certain feelings because they are "bad" will only prolong or abort the discipleship process needed for long-term transformation in our lives.

## Week 6: Discover the Rhythms of the Daily Office and Sabbath

[16]Be sure not to spend too much time here. Realistically, there is only time for 2-3 people to share in a 10-minute period

[17]The leader/facilitator will want to read this thoughtfully and slowly.

[18]This is a learned practice that takes time. For some it will be difficult; for others it will not be long enough. Others will struggle with all their interior noise. Be ready for a wide variety of responses. Hopefully, many will have adjusted comfortably to the rhythm of the Daily Office if they have been doing it since your small group began.

[19]The concept of the Daily Office has a rich history going back to Daniel, David, the Jews during the time of Jesus, and the early church. It is the rhythm of stopping to be with God at set times during the day so that we can "practice the presence of God."

[20]God modeled for us working six days and resting one. We have managed to turn our "days off" from work into work days as well, filling them with activities (e.g. chores, finishing our "to do" lists, etc). We don't actually stop to rest, delight and contemplate God.

## Week 7: Grow into an Emotionally Mature Adult

[21]Be aware this can lead to a lively discussion! The following are examples of possible answers: We often emphasize spiritual productivity and gifts, often overlooking troublesome character traits. We also equate the knowledge of Scripture to spiritual maturity and ignore emotional immaturity. Loving well is much more difficult to measure than content and doing ministry for God. So be prepared to end this discussion in the time allotted and move on to the next section.

[22]For a fuller discussion of Martin Buber's distinction between "I-It" and "I-Thou" relationships, see Scazzero, *Emotionally Healthy Spirituality*, 181–183.

[23]It is important that we maintain the creative tension and healthy balance between self-care and self-giving. Living at either extreme leads us to eventually resent people or ignore those in need around us altogether. The Samaritan stops to help the hurting man. At the same time, he has the self-awareness and self-respect to recognize his own limits and decides to resume his own journey the next day. A healthy balance of self-care

and self-giving in our lives is necessary in order to live out an "I-Thou" relationship both toward ourselves and others.

[24]This exercise is adapted from Pan Ennis, *The Third Option: Ministry to Hurting Marriages*, Teachers Manual, Topic #3, "Expectations," 1-9.

[25]Avoid examples of expectations around moral issues or responsibilities (e.g. domestic abuse, adultery, parent's role in nurturing children, financial integrity in our church). These issues go beyond the scope of this exercise.

## Week 8: Go the Next Step to Develop a Rule of Life

[26]Please note that this Bible Study is very intentionally only fifteen minutes. We have placed the weight of this final meeting on the application exercise for which they will need 45 minutes.

[27]Remember, a Rule of Life is simply an intentional, conscious plan to keep God at the center of everything we do. It provides guidelines to help us continually remember God as the source of our lives. It includes our unique combination of spiritual practices that provide structure and direction for us to intentionally pay attention and remember God in everything we do.

[28]Notice that there is no hint of legalism or "shoulds" in the description of the church in Acts. Jesus said "My yoke is easy and my burden is light. (Matthew 11:28–30). In the same way, any healthy rule of life we develop needs to fit how God made us at this particular season of our life.

[29]This exercise is best done in giving the members physical space to be alone. If space allows, have the individual members find a personal spot where they can spend these fifteen minutes in solitude contemplating these questions before God.

C3 80

## Emotionally Healthy Spirituality DVD

We strongly encourage you to use this important tool with this *Emotionally Healthy Spirituality Workbook*. The DVD includes:

- A 6–10 minute introduction by Peter Scazzero of each of the eight sessions that your small group views together.

- Instructions for leaders by Pete to help facilitate each of the eight sessions.

Available for sale on our Web site.

## Sermon Series
## Begin the Journey into Emotionally Healthy Spirituality

This nine-part series was originally preached at New Life Fellowship Church by Pete Scazzero during a church wide initiative integrating the powerful principles of Emotionally Healthy Spirituality into the life of the church. These weekly messages further supplement the themes of the book and workbook with an even broader biblical foundation.

1. The Problem of Emotionally Unhealthy Spirituality (1 Sam. 15:7-24)
2. Know Yourself that You May Know God (1 Sam. 17:26-45)
3. Going Back in Order to Go Forward (Gen. 50:15-21)
4. Journey Through the Wall (Gen.22:1-14)
5. Enlarge Your Soul Through Grief and Loss (Matt. 26:31-44)
6. Discover the Rhythms of the Daily Office and Sabbath (Dan.6:6-10)
7. Grow into an Emotionally Mature Adult (Luke 10:25-37)
8. Go the Next Step to Develop a "Rule of Life" (Acts 2:42-47)
9. Summary and Application — Daily Office and Testimonies

Available for sale on our Web site.

**Visit our Web site to purchase these items,
for additional resources,
or for information about Emotionally Healthy Spirituality**

## www.emotionallyhealthy.org